WORLD WAR TWO
SOLDIERS

Laurent MIROUZE

HISTOIRE & COLLECTIONS

POLISH INFANTRYMAN, SEPTEMBER 1939

At the end of World War I, Poland regained her independence as a sovereign state. Her army was made up of many contingents originally raised, equipped and armed by the different belligerent nations of 1914-18. At the beginning of the 1930s the army's first efforts at uniformity were overtaken by a radical new issue of uniforms, equipment and weapons, selected after wide-ranging trials. The new brown uniforms were notably modern in design; the individual equipment was partly derived from the current German army equivalents. But the 39 Polish infantry divisions were unable to resist for long the German steamroller which smashed through Poland's borders in September 1939. After three heroic weeks, their resistance – partly undermined by Russia's treacherous agreement to partition Poland with Germany – was beaten down.

1 - M1931 **helmet**, in nickel/chrome molybdenum steel, painted in a brown-green shade, with powdered cork added to the paint to produce a dull finish known as 'Salamander.' The leather lining, one of the most advanced designs of the period, was derived from that of the old German M1916, with small adjustable pads to adjust the fit.

2 - The M1936 **tunic** was of a single pattern for all ranks, in brown wool. The silver buttons bear the 1927 crowned eagle national emblem. The garment features four patch pockets with buttoned flap. In service dress, rank insignia and unit ciphers were displayed on the shoulder straps; the collar bore patches in branch colours, with the traditional Polish zig-zag silver braid. For field dress, as here, only rank insignia was retained.

3 - Universal issue M1936 **belt**, in tan leather with a single-prong buckle.

4 - Two 1919 pattern triple **cartridge pouches** in tan leather, modelled on the German WW1 design. Each pocket held three five-round clips of 7.9 mm ammunition, giving a total of 90 rounds.

5 - **Entrenching tool** in tan leather carrier, to which was secured the leather M1931 bayonet frog, which accommodated different types of bayonet then in Polish army use; the one illustrated is the M1927.

6 - M1933 **haversack** in proofed brown canvas. It could be carried either slung on the left side, or attached to the right side of the belt. Normal contents were the waterbottle, washing kit and small personal effects, emergency rations, and a hand grenade.

7 - M1932 **knapsack**, of heavy canvas, its shoulder straps linked to the cartridge pouches at the front. External stowage comprised the rolled greatcoat and blanket, and sometimes a tent section strapped round the sides, and the aluminium mess tin of German pattern (8) strapped to the flap. The tent section was sometimes carried inside the pack, with a change of underclothes, shirt and socks, laces, rifle cleaning kit, etc.

9 - M1932 **gasmask** in its canvas bag; some troops still carried the WW1 French ARS mask, which the Polish type was in the process of replacing at the outbreak of war.

10 - M1937 wool **trousers**, of the same shade as the tunic, gathered at the ankle by buttoned wool anklets (11).

12 - M1934 **ankle boots** in natural tan leather; regulations of 1935 had prescribed that these should normally be blacked, but many were still in their natural finish. Unlike most contemporary military boots, their soles were screwed on, rather than sewn, and thus gave superior protection against damp.

13 - M1929 Mauser pattern **rifle**, a Polish variant of the classic German weapon. Of 7.9 mm calibre, it was manufactured in government arsenals at Warsaw and Radom. Many captured rifles were salvaged for use by the Wehrmacht after the Polish defeat.

GERMAN INFANTRYMAN, FRANCE, MAY - JUNE 1940

The outlook of the German soldier of 1940 represented the final stage in the evolution of the field grey uniform which first appeared in 1907. Since the establishment of the Reichsheer in 1919, the uniform had been identical for all German states. A new field tunic appeared in 1935, together with a new helmet, but individual equipment still derived from WW1 items. In accordance with Hitler's wishes the smartness of the uniform was enhanced by the adoption of a richly varied system of emblems and badges. In May - June 1940 the 'Landser' was a formidable opponent, well armed and equipped, and provided with transport which made possible the fast-moving 'Blitzkrieg' which gained Germany her first great victories.

1 - M1935 **helmet**; of 1.2 mm-thick steel, it was painted dull slate grey. The M1931 lining comprised leather segments mounted on an adjustable ring. Originally, army helmets bore two decals: a tricolour shield (black, white, red), and a silver-grey eagle upon a black shield. From May 1940, the new slate grey paint finish was supposed to be applied over the tricolour shield, and only the eagle remained.

2 - M1933 tunic collar liner, attached by five buttons. It was reversible, white cotton on one side and green on the other, the former being exposed with walking-out uniform and the latter with field dress. By regulation, a centimetre's height was supposed to show above the collar.

3 - Removable **shoulder straps**, the examples illustrated being of the type made in the period 1938-40. In dark green 'insignia' cloth with a white piping for the infantry, they bore the regimental cipher in the pre-war period. After the outbreak of war, the ciphers were either covered by a cloth loop, or omitted during manufacture, for obvious reasons of security.

4 - M1935 field grey **tunic**, fastening with five buttons down the front, and provided with four pleated pockets fastened by buttoned flaps. The collar, of dark blueish green 'insignia' cloth, bore two patches, their design being a simplified form of traditional Prussian collar lace, with arm of service colour median stripes. Before the introduction of the M1939 leather equipment suspenders, the tunic had inner fabric suspenders linked to belt hooks protruding through eyelets in the cloth to help support the leather belt. Above the right breast pocket was sewn the national emblem of an eagle clutching a wreathed swastika. Rank chevrons identifying junior NCOs – here those of a senior corporal – were sewn to the left sleeve only.

5 - Oilcloth pouch for the **gas cape**, secured to the gasmask sling or canister.

6 - M1933 **cartridge pouches**, in two sets of three, each set containing 6 five-round clips of 7.92 mm caliber rounds. The pouches were of black leather with a pebbled finish.

7 - **Gasmask canister** M1930, in fluted metal painted grey-green.

8 - Black leather **bayonet frog**, with M1884-98 rifle bayonet.

9 - **Entrenching tool** in its artificial leather carrier, whose strap both holds the head of the tool and the bayonet scabbard to keep it from flapping around.

10 - M1931 **tent section**/shelter half. The 'Zeltbahn,' in proofed cotton cloth with a three-tone camouflage pattern on both sides, is roughly triangular. It has a central slit for the head, and can be worn as a poncho, or buttoned to others to fashion a field shelter.

11 - M1931 **bread bag** in olive canvas. Its regulation contents included: washing kit, weapon cleaning kit, emergency rations, eating utensils, field cap, etc.

12 - M1931 **mess tin**, of grey-green painted aluminum.

13 - The M1931 **water bottle**, with a capacity of roughly 1.2 pint, is covered with felt, and has a black-painted aluminium cup fixed over the neck.

14 - Stone grey wool **trousers**. These feature two slash side pockets closed by buttons, one right rear pocket and one small fob pocket in the right front.

15 - Black leather marching **boots**.

16 - Mauser pattern Karabiner 98k **rifle**, 7.92 mm calibre.

An M1924 stick **grenade** is slipped into the left boot shaft.

FRENCH INFANTRYMAN, FRANCE, MAY - JUNE 1940

When the French army mobilised in September 1939, infantry soldiers could have walked out of a 1918 photograph, with the sole major difference of wearing brown wool rather than horizon blue. The image of the victor of the Great War, familiar from a thousand bronze war memorials, seemed stamped into the military mentality. The equipment, which had been criticised since the turn of the century, had certainly been the subject of a number of spot reforms: M1935 equipment with a knapsack of soft canvas rather than rigidly framed material; MAS36 rifle; M1938 uniform. But although these innovations had been partially introduced by the spring of 1940, the French foot-slogger still faced the light, mobile German infantry weighed down by a heavy greatcoat recalling the Franco-Prussian War, and a bulky and over-complex harness.

1 - The manganese steel M1926 **helmet** followed the general form of the 1915 'Adrian' helmet. The front badge varied according to the branch of service; for the infantry it was a flaming grenade.

2 - M1935 shirt and tie. The soldier could also wear a light sweater (M1936) under the greatcoat, but not a tunic. This had been withdrawn from field dress in 1937 in an effort to lighten the soldier's load.

3 - Greatcoat M1920/35, double-breasted, with two rows of six brown finished buttons. The new M1938 greatcoat, single-breasted with five buttons, had been issued to some troops by this date. The collar patches bear the regimental number and two dark blue infantry stripes. Note also the yellow and green fourragère awarded to the 69th Fortress Infantry Regiment, and the 1939 Croix de Guerre awarded to this soldier. A single rolled shoulder strap, designed to prevent equipment straps from slipping, is attached on the right side. The regulations called for two.

4 - M1935 individual equipment. Designed as an integrated set of items, it represented a real improvement over the old equipment with its rigid wood-framed knapsack, and its plethora of equipment slings crossing on the chest. Unfortunately, only about one third of the French infantry had received the new system by spring 1940. It incorporated the standard leather belt (M1903/14) and suspenders (M1892/14).

5 - Two M1935/37 **cartridge pouches** were carried at the front of the belt, for a total of 90 rounds. The third pouch of the old equipment, carried at the back, was replaced by a triangular leather loop which engaged with the rear strap of the suspender system.

6 - The 1935 pattern **water bottle** held about 3.2 pints.

7 - M1935 **haversack**, normally containing the mess tins and cup, eating utensils, daily rations, and additional magazines for the section light machine gun.

8 - M1935 **knapsack**, containing reserve rations, washing kit and housewife, wool sweater, short blanket, field cap, etc. The side pockets could accommodate light machine gun magazines. A lower pack – not illustrated here – could be attached below the knapsack, and held spare clothing.

9 - The **tent section** M1935, square in shape, had a central slit allowing it to be worn as a poncho.

10 - Entrenching tool, here the M1916 shovel, in the M1935 leather carrier.

11 - ANP31 **gas mask** in its bag. Like the British model, it had a tube connecting the mask to a filter which remained in the bag.

12 - M1938 trousers, also called 'golf trousers,' they reflected contemporary fashion in bagginess, but were less than satisfactory in the field, and tore easily. In 1940 about half the infantry still wore the M1920/35 breeches-trousers, gathered at the knee.

13 - High wool **puttees**. Although laced gaiters were put into production in 1940, few reached the troops before the Armistice.

14 - Hobnailed M1917 **ankle boots**.

15 - 1907/15 M16 Berthier **rifle**, in 8-mm Lebel calibre. Nicknamed the 'fishing rod' because of its length, this old weapon still equipped the majority of the infantry in 1940, alongside with the shorter M16 carbine variant. The long cruciform bayonet was carried on the left side of the belt, and is hidden here by the turnback of the greatcoat.

SCOTTISH INFANTRYMAN, FRANCE, FEBRUARY 1940

This private of the Argyll and Sutherland Highlanders, who landed in France in January 1940 during the freezing but relatively inactive winter of the 'Phoney War,' differs little in general appearance from his predecessors of 1918. Despite the introduction of new items of uniform and equipment from 1937 onwards, the traditional attributes of the Highland soldier are still represented. After the arrival of the British Expeditionary Force in France, orders were issued banning the issue of the kilt to troops going overseas. But photographs show that the 'Jocks' clung to their traditional uniform for a while, despite its unsuitability for modern warfare. The 51st Highland Division suffered terrible losses in the course of the bitter retreat to the Channel. The 7th Argylls were almost wiped out, and the survivors finally went into captivity after a heroic last stand near Saint-Valéry-en-Caux.

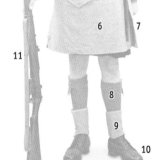

1 - Tam o'Shanter **bonnet** in brown serge, with the regimental badge pinned through a patch of distinctive '42d Government' pattern tartan on the left side.

2 - Battledress blouse. The original model, as here, had all buttons concealed by flies except for those on the shoulder strap. Regulations forbidding the display of insignia in the field were at this time generally obeyed, although not universally. The use of an improvised scarf may appear unconvincing, but at least one photograph of Highlanders taken at this time confirms it; the flannel shirt was collarless, and the neck of the rough serge blouse chafed the skin.

3 - Steel **helmet** Mk II, painted semi-matt green or brown. The chin strap and lining had been improved since WWI; the shell was less obviously modified, the brim being flatter and the dome circular rather than ovoid.

4 - The Service respirator (**gasmask**), here in the 'alert' position, hung from the neck by an adjustable strap and held against the chest by a length of string. The rubber face piece was attached by a corrugated rubber tube to the filter cartridge, which remained in its pocket inside the bag when the mask was put on.

5 - 1937 pattern **individual equipment** in cotton webbing. The various items were all linked, in an attempt to spread their weight. Supported by both the belt and the suspenders are a pair of 'basic pouches': each could accommodate either a cotton bandolier of 50 rounds for the .303 rifle and a couple of hand grenades, or two magazines for the section's Bren light machine gun, or two bombs for the platoon's 2 in. mortar. The wool-covered enamelled water bottle also buckled to the free ends of the suspenders, carried down through buckles on the belt.

6 - Kilt, in 42nd (Government) sett for the Argylls, and drab cloth kilt cover. However, by late Spring 1940, most if not all Highlanders in Maj. Gen. Fortune's 51st Division wore Battledress trousers.

7 - Bayonet No 1 Mk I; this new nomenclature was applied to the basically identical sword bayonet carried since before the Great War.

8 - Hose tops: footless stockings worn in addition to the issue socks by kilted units, the turned-down tops traditionally decorated with garter flashes in regimental colours.

9 - Webbing anklets, reinforced with leather patches inside and fastened by two buckled straps, they replaced the old puttees with the introduction of the 1937 uniform and equipment.

10 - 'Ammunition boots,' sturdily made in pebbled and blackened leather, and heavily hob-nailed.

11 - Rifle No1 Mk III*. The Short Magazine Lee Enfield of .303in. calibre was the mainstay of the British army since the Great War. This bolt-action weapon, with a removable magazine holding ten rounds, was robust and reliable, and in the hands of trained troops, capable of accurate and surprisingly rapid fire.

BELGIAN INFANTRYMAN, MAY-JUNE 1940

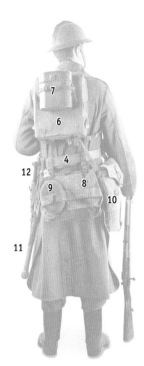

In 1915 the Belgian army adapted itself, for better or worse, to trench warfare, discarding its gaudy uniforms for a less conspicuous brown outfit supplied from British sources. With the adoption of the Adrian helmet, the Belgian soldier, who also wore a greatcoat with turned-back skirts, acquired a very French appearance, which had changed little by 1940. The new 1935 uniform only incorporated slight modifications of the Great War pattern. The individual equipment, introduced shortly after 1918, followed the general outlines of the German equivalent: triple ammunition pouches, haversack, slung water bottle, etc. At the time of Belgian mobilisation some troops were issued with the M1915 Mills equipment. Like his French comrade, the Belgian infantryman faced the fast-moving Wehrmacht in an outfit too heavy and cumbersome for modern warfare.

1 - M1931 **helmet** in manganese steel, painted brown, an almost exact copy of the French M1926, apart from the more horizontal angle of the brim at front and back, and the black leather lining. The front bore the lion-head emblem of the Belgian army for all branches of service.

2 - Brown wool M1922 **greatcoat**, with two rows of five large buttons bearing the lion device. It had two side pockets with straight buttoned flaps, and two vertical rear pockets below the half-belt. There is a bottom vent at the back; in marching order, as illustrated, the fronts were buttoned back to free the legs. The grenade insignia on the collar identify a regiment of Grenadiers, and the shoulder straps bear the regimental cipher below a small grenade. In the Belgian army, the tunic was worn under the greatcoat.

3 - Cotton **collar**, giving some protection against the chafing of the heavy coat cloth.

4 - Tan **leather belt** with adjustable buckle; personal variations were not uncommon.

5 - Tan leather **ammunition pouches**, each of the three pockets holding three five-round clips, giving a total capacity of 90 rounds.

6 - M1930 **knapsack**, made of thick greenish canvas over a bamboo frame, with leather shoulder straps and webbing stowage straps. Four loops on the flap allowed the attachment of the mess tin as illustrated; straps on the sides secured the rolled blanket and spare boots.

7 - **Mess tin** in brown painted aluminium, with strap loops on each side.

8 - **Musette bag**, 1930 pattern, copied from the German bread bag, with external fittings for one or two water bottles. Made of brown canvas, it could be slipped on the belt or slung thanks to a long strap. It contained rations and spare clothing.

9 - Aluminium **water bottle** (capacity 1 liter) covered in brown wool cloth, with a cork stopper. A leather strap sewn to the cover allowed it to be attached to the rear bag.

10 - 1924 pattern **gas mask**, carried in a slung bag. Like the British model, the rubber face piece was attached by a tube to the filter cartridge carried permanently in the satchel.

11 - Linneman type **entrenching tool** in its tan leather carrier. There were several models, often with a strap holding the bayonet scabbard to the tool in the German fashion.

12 - Tan leather **bayonet frog** and M1916/35 bayonet, its hilt secured by a strap.

13 - 1935 pattern brown **wool trousers**, straight-cut, with two slanted side pockets and a right rear pocket. The trousers were supported by braces.

14 - Black **leather gaiters**, laced up the front by means of seven metal hooks.

15 - Blackened leather ankle **boots**.

16 - M35 Mauser pattern **rifle** of 7.65 mm calibre. As in many smaller armies of the period, this was a nationally manufactured version of the German rifle.

ITALIAN MOUNTAIN TROOPER, JUNE 1940

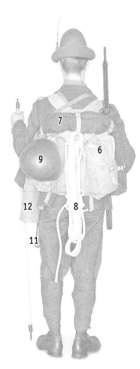

I n 1940, six of the Italian army's 73 divisions were of the 'Alpine' type. The establishment of these special troops had been a natural response to Italy's rugged terrain, and particularly to the fact that her northern frontier passes through some of the greatest mountain massifs in Europe. The uniform of the 'Alpini' differed little from that of the other troops except in their headgear and insignia. They also received specialised equipment in the form of cleated boots, a Tyrolian-style rucksack, the Alpenstock, climbing ropes and crampons, etc. Considered as crack soldiers, the Alpini were committed against France's own mountain troops during Mussolini's pointless campaign of 10-25 June 1940 - a stab in the back of a country already locked in desperate battle against the German invaders, and a campaign which produced meagre results due to inadequate leadership and logistics.

1 - The felt Alpine **hat**, introduced in 1910 and still in use today. The jaunty trademark of the Alpini was reluctantly laid aside for the steel helmet in combat. The black crow's feather was affixed by a tuft in battalion colour: white for the 1st Bn. in each regiment, red for the 2nd, green for the 3rd and blue for the 4th. The front badge, embroidered in black thread on grey-green cloth, consisted of a flying eagle over a bugle-horn and crossed rifles. In the curl of the bugle-horn the regimental number was displayed, here, the 3rd.

2 - M1939 **shirt**, in grey-green flannel or lighter material according to the season, and universal issue throughout the army. It had two breast pockets, and a two-button front vent down to mid-chest level. It was often worn with a tie, normally grey-green but of different colours in certain units.

3 - M1940 **tunic**, in the grey-green shade adopted for Italian army uniforms in 1909. This four-pocket, open collar design was common to most branches of service; note the integral cloth belt with two buttons. Junior NCOs' sleeve rank insignia were embroidered in red on a grey-green ground - here, the chevrons of a corporal. Arm-of-service collar patches were in distinctive colours, and shaped as two- or three-point flames. These are green for mountain troops, with the white metal star of Savoy which appeared on all Italian army collar patches.

4 - M1891 **belt** of grey-green leather, its single prong buckle placed on the side to permit the wearing of the ammunition pouches centrally at the front.

5 - M1907 double **cartridge pouch** in grey-green leather, each pocket holding four clips of 6.5 mm ammunition for the Carcano rifle. The weight was partly supported by the M1891 suspender, which passed round the neck.

6 - M1939 mountain troops **rucksack**, in heavy canvas. This capacious pack has two large exterior pockets, and five fabric straps to attach the greatcoat,

blanket, and/or a tent section in camouflage material. This very popular pack was sometimes issued to regular infantry formations.

7 - Grey-green wool single-breasted **greatcoat**, rolled and tied around the pack in regulation fashion.

8 - Climbing **rope**.

9 - M1933 steel **helmet**, painted grey-green, bearing the stencilled badge of the Alpini and the regimental number. The helmet was sometimes seen with a side fixture for the Alpine troops' traditional tuft and feather.

10 - **Water bottle**, in aluminium covered with grey green cloth; it was issued in one-litre and two-litre capacity, the larger type being illustrated here.

11 - **Bayonet** frog and M1891 **entrenching tool** carrier, here containing a combination pick/shovel.

12 - Model T35 **gasmask**, carried in a cylindrical cloth bag, the size being marked in Roman numerals on the outside of the bag.

13 - Ash wood M1934 **Alpenstock**.

14 - M1940 grey-green **trousers**, in the full, straight, ankle-length cut issued to Alpine troops.

15 - Standard **puttees**.

16 - M1912 mountain **boots**, with climbing cleats.

17 - M1891 Carcano **rifle** in 6.5 mm calibre.

AFRIKAKORPS INFANTRYMAN, LIBYA, FEBRUARY 1941

Responding to the pleas of his Italian allies, repeatedly and expensively defeated by the British in North Africa, Hitler assembled and despatched an expeditionary corps, which disembarked at Tripoli in February 1941. The German army's experience of tropical campaigning was limited to minor colonial operations long before, and they faced the task of preparing from scratch for a new and challenging theatre of operations. Responsibility for designing a new uniform was given to the Hamburg Tropical Institute. Under pressure of time, the Institute supposedly chose to take the British army in India as its model; but if so, the wrong lessons were drawn. The uniform worn by the Afrikakorps in their first battles consisted of a sun helmet, a cotton tunic, cut rather too snugly for comfort; and half-breeches resembling jodhpurs. This outfit was quickly modified in the light of desert experience, and more loose-fitting and practical alternatives were found.

1 - M1940 tropical **helmet** in cork covered with olive cloth. A painted metal shield was pinned to each side, echoing the decals of the steel helmet: on the right, the national colours, and on the left the eagle and swastika emblem of the Heer (Army).

2 - Tropical **shirt** in olive green cotton, with a four-button front and two large breast pockets.

3 - **Tie** in olive green cotton, hardly ever seen in the front line.

4 - Removable **shoulder straps**, made in the same cloth as the uniform, with the usual arm-of-service colour piping. Rose pink identified armoured units, including motorised troops within the Panzer divisions.

5 - M1940 **tropical tunic** in olive green canvas. It was similar in cut to the wool tunic, but with an open collar and dull blue and brown woven collar tabs, with no variation between branches of service. The national eagle above the right breast was also woven in blue on brown. The left breast bears the bronze armoured units assault badge awarded to participants in at least three actions. At this stage of the war, the motorised troops and armour crews of the Panzer divisions shared the same design.

6 - Shoulder **suspenders** for the infantry, in yellowish webbing, apart from a round leather tab at the point of junction high on the back. Various hooks and rings allowed the suspenders to be connected to the ammunition pouches and belt, and the attachment of the assault pack on the back.

7 - Standard issue **ammunition pouches**.

8 - Webbing version of the standard **bayonet frog**.

9 - M1884/98 **bayonet**.

10 - Webbing **belt**, its buckle being painted in dark olive green.

11 - **Entrenching tool**, here in the standard issue black leather carrier.

12 - Webbing **assault pack frame**, hooked onto the equipment suspenders. Several straps allowed for the attachment of various combinations of kit. Here the M1931 mess tin is carried above the rolled M1931 camouflaged Zeltbahn, and the special cloth satchel under it holds a sweater, rations, tent pegs, and rifle cleaning kit.

13 - M1931 **bread bag**. Apart from the normal contents, the bag would accommodate the peaked tropical field cap in olive green canvas.

14 - Tropical **water bottle**, made of aluminium covered with a compound of vulcanised fibre and wood, which gave better insulation against tropical heat. For the same reason, the cup fitted over the neck was made of bakelite.

15 - M1940 olive green cotton tropical **breeches**, laced at the calf; they have two slanted slash side pockets and a front fob pocket.

16 - High laced leather and canvas tropical **boots**; this obsolete design was soon generally abandoned in favour of ankle boots of the same materials.

17 - Karabiner 98k **rifle**, 7.92 mm calibre.

© Histoire & Collections

12

13   14

BRITISH NCO, WESTERN DESERT, SPRING 1942

This NCO of the 50th (Northumbrian) Division represents an 8th Army soldier at the time of Rommel's May/June offensive against the Gazala Line. Although lightened, his equipment is made up from the same range of items as worn in the other main theatres of operations. His clothing owes much to pre-war experience in India, where the current field dress had been khaki drill shorts, the old 'greyback' shirt, and a khaki sweater for cool nights. During the 1930s the 'greyback' was replaced by a khaki loose weave 'Aertex' shirt. This uniform - or Battledress, in cold weather, which was far from unknown in North Africa - was worn throughout the African campaign.

1 - Mark II steel **helmet** painted in sand-colour.

2 - Aertex **shirt**, made of a loose-weave material for coolness. Cut with long tails, it had two pleated breast pockets, and a four-button pullover front. It was always worn open at the neck. Because shirts were washed as often as practical, insignia were not permanently attached. Chevrons of rank – in standard form, or in plain white tape – were temporarily attached either with press studs or hooks and eyes, and often to the right sleeve only. The divisional sign of the 50th Division is sewn on removable shoulder strap slides.

3 - 1937 pattern **webbing equipment**. In North Africa it was scrubbed, and lengthy exposure to the sun could bleach it almost white. The combination illustrated was for personnel not issued with the rifle or light machine gun: the suspenders attach directly to the belt by means of brass and webbing connectors. The water bottle is carried in the back. Our NCO has arranged his equipment to personal taste.

4 - M1928 Thompson **sub-machine gun**, with 50-round drum magazine. Ordered in large quantities from the USA in 1940, it was the standard sub-machine gun until the general issue of the lighter and cheaper Sten 'machine carbine' and was still seen in use by 8th Army units in Italy quite late in the war, since its heavy .45 calibre round and greater reliability were preferred. No item of the 1937 equipment was designed to carry the large drum magazines, which were later generally discarded in favour of the box magazine which fitted into the basic pouch. Therefore, our NCO carries them in his slung haversack. The haversack, or 'small pack' usually held the mess tins and utensils, washing kit and housewife, a sweater, emergency ration tin, and - theoretically - the water bottle.

5 - Enfield No. 2 Mark I 38 in. **revolver**. This was not normally carried by junior ranks of infantry, except for medium machine gun crews. This NCO, commanding a section of ten men, has 'scrounged' one as a secondary weapon of last resort. He has fitted the 1937 pattern webbing holster to the bottom of the pistol cartridge pouch, and the pouch to the belt. The regulation arrangement was to fit the pouch on the left suspender, above the holster mounted on the belt, butt forwards. The pistol was retained by a neck lanyard.

6 - Khaki drill **shorts**, cut very full. The waist was adjusted by two cotton straps and metal buckles. The pocket on the front held the First field dressing.

7 - Long **socks** or hose tops gave some protection from sun, dust and flies.

8 - Short **puttees** gave some support to the ankle, and prevented sand getting down into the boot.

9 - Standard issue hobnailed 'Ammunition' **boots**.

ITALIAN INFANTRYMAN, WESTERN DESERT, 1942

I taly's entry into the war in June 1940 was a gamble. Mussolini was aware of his country's unpreparedness for war against modern European enemies, but he feared that Italy would be left out of the division of spoils if Germany won a quick and easy victory, as then seemed likely. Early moves against British colonies in East Africa and at the Libyan/Egyptian border were accompanied by an invasion of Greece. In all these campaigns large but ill-prepared Italian armies suffered almost immediate and costly set-backs at the hands of smaller enemy forces. Catastrophic reverses in Greece and North Africa forced Germany to come to her ally's aid. But large Italian forces continued to fight alongside the Afrikakorps throughout 1941-42; relatively short of transport and effective armour and air support, they generally provided the infantry mass, while Rommel's mobile divisions provided the 'punch.' The Axis defeat in North Africa in spring 1943, followed by the Allied invasion of Sicily, led to the overthrow of the Fascist government and Italy's conclusion of a unilateral armistice with the Allies in September.

1 - M1935 pith **helmet** as worn by other ranks. It bears the brass infantry device superimposed on a tricolour cockade in red/white/green.

2 - Late-model sun and dust **goggles.**

3 - A **bush jacket**, the stylish 'Sahariana,' was worn widely as an alternative to the lightweight cotton version of the woollen M1940 tunic. It is identifiable by its stand and fall collar, and by the large yoke covering the shoulders. The collar patches are those of the 'Bologna' Division, comprising the 39th and 40th Infantry and 205th Artillery Regiments, which fought at Alamein under XXI Italian Corps.

4 - The **trousers**, in matching material, were of the same cut as the M1940 woollen garment. They were gathered below the knee by laces, and confined by puttees, as often as not of grey-green wool cloth.

5 - M1912 natural leather **hobnailed boots.**

6 - M1907 double **cartridge pouches** in grey-green leather, each pocket holding four clips of 6.5 mm rounds for the Carcano M1891/38 rifle or carbine. The pouch rig was standard issue on all fronts, despite its inconvenience when the soldier had to lie prone.

7 - M1891 **bayonet** in its metal scabbard, carried in a grey-green leather frog.

8 - T35 **gasmask** in its carrier.

9 - Water bottle of standard pattern, in aluminium covered with grey-green wool, on an adjustable sling. The mouthpiece has a valve which allows a thin trickle of water to be released - theoretically, an aid to water economy in the field, though one may doubt that it had much practical effect in the hands of troops.

10 - Haversack, stowed with the rolled greatcoat on top and with a sand coloured tent section underneath. This was however less frequently seen than the M1929 camouflaged model.

11 - M1891 Carcano **rifle** in 6.5 mm calibre.

FRENCH FOREIGN LEGIONNAIRE, WESTERN DESERT, 1942

At the time of the French Armistice in June 1940 several thousand French soldiers and sailors found themselves on British soil. Notable among these were the troops led by General Béthouart, withdrawn from Norway after the Narvik campaign. They faced a crucial choice: whether to accept the Armistice and return to occupied France and their families; or whether to fight on under the entirely new colours of the Free French, in a war whose outcome could only be guessed. Most of the Chasseurs Alpins and sailors chose to return home; but more than half of the Foreign Legion's 13e Demi-Brigade elected to fight on under General De Gaulle. For these légionnaires, a long and extraordinary crusade was just beginning. From 1940 to 1943 the légionnaires, like the rest of the Free French, were supplied from British sources. But they made every effort to keep their traditional distinctions. From the summer of 1943, when the Free French Forces and the French Army in Africa came together after the defeat of the Axis forces in Tunisia, they formed the French Army of Liberation, and were re-equipped with American uniforms, equipment and weapons.

1 - The **white-topped képi** was the distinctive headgear of the Legion. It was in fact a regulation képi, with a dark blue body and a crimson top, fitted with a white sun cover. Originally this had been khaki, but the desert sun and frequent washing bleached it white. A gold lace false chin strap was worn by senior corporals and sergeants.

2 - Another traditional item was the 'chèche,' the **desert scarf** of the Sahara camel troops. By the outbreak of war, this long piece of khaki muslin had become a regulation item for African and motorised units.

3 - By the time Gen. Koenig's 1st Free French Brigade won fame at Bir Hakeim, the Legion had long since received both **Battledress** and Khaki Drill clothing from the British. The 13e DBLE added to the BD blouse the Free French emblem - the Cross of Lorraine - on the sleeve, and Foreign Legion dark blue collar patches, with two green pipings and the seven-flamed grenade, in green for other ranks and gold for senior NCOs.

4 - Old pattern French **individual equipment**, issued for the Norwegian campaign. It comprised of the standard M1903/14 belt, M1892/14 suspenders, three M1916 cartridge pouches, a two-litre M1935 water bottle and sling, and a light brown sidebag used for rations and small kit.

5 - British **KD shorts**, of the type popularly known as 'Bombay bloomers.' The buttoned legs could be unfolded and tucked into long socks, as protection against sun, insects and blister gas. They were hardly ever so worn, in practice.

6 - British **hose tops**, often worn rolled down over the top of the boot by the French.

7 - French M1917 **ankle boots**.

8 - French MAS 36 **rifle** in 7.5 mm calibre, issued to some infantry and all cavalry units shortly before the outbreak of war. As with other modern items of equipment, it was the mainstay of the Norway expeditionary force. The long needle-bayonet fitted beneath the barrel when not fixed, so was not carried on the belt.

ITALIAN INFANTRYMAN, ITALY, 1942

The uniform and equipment of the World War II Italian infantry did not differ markedly from those of the Great War. The uniform remained 'grigio-verde,' the grey-green colour adopted in 1909. Successive regulations altered points of detail, but the overall appearance of the soldier hardly changed in 30 years; the only major innovation was the introduction of an open-collar tunic in 1933. The new uniform issued from 1940 onward was made of a wool and artificial fiber material, and was worn in all climates except the African desert. Individual equipment remained unchanged. As for their small arms, the Italians made a tentative effort to replace the 6.5 mm calibre, that had proved inadequate in Ethiopia and Spain. But after going some way towards introducing new weapons in 7.35 mm, they reverted to the old calibre rather than face the difficulty and expense of re-equipping an expanding army then mobilising for war. The range of infantry weapons and calibres which actually saw service proved a nightmare for the logistic services.

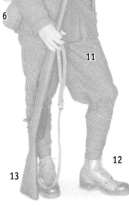

1 - M1933 nickel-steel **helmet**, painted dull grey-green; it has three ventilation holes, and up to 1942 the branch-of-service badge was stencilled on the front in black paint.

2 - M1939 **shirt**, of grey-green flannel for winter and lighter cloth for summer wear. It had a fall collar, for use with a necktie of the same shade; two buttoned breast pockets; and a two-button pullover front.

3 - M1940 open-collar **tunic** in grey-green semi-synthetic material. It had four buttoned patch pockets, and an integral cloth belt with two adjustment buttons. Unlike the former pattern, whose collar was in the branch colours, the 1940 tunic was grey green all over. On the sleeve is the red double chevron of a corporal, worn on both arms. The collar patches varied in colours and shape depending upon the branch of service and the formation: these white rectangles identify the 50th Division 'Regina,' composed of the 9th, 10th, 309th and 331st Infantry Regiments. The silver star of Savoy was worn on army collar patches by all ranks.

4 - M1891 individual **equipment**, of leather chemically dyed greyish green. The neck suspender hooked behind the cartridge pouches; the narrow belt was worn with the buckle offset to the left.

5 - M1907 double **cartridge pouches**, each pocket holding four clips of 6.5 mm Carcano ammunition.

6 - Standard issue **water bottle** in cloth-covered aluminium; one- and two- litre sizes were issued according to branch of service.

7 - M1939 **haversack** in heavy canvas with leather straps. Il had three interior compartments; and the external straps held the rolled greatcoat, blanket, and M1929 camouflaged tent section, the latter also serving as a poncho.

8 - M1933 **gasmask** bag, used as a sidebag for small kit since the introduction of the newer T35 mask.

9 - **Mess tin**, made in aluminium since 1930. Of oval shape, it could be strapped directly onto the sidebag or, as here, in its own cover.

10 - M1891 **bayonet frog**, secured to the entrenching tool carrier. This latter could accommodate several different tools - here, a shovel.

11 - Grey-green **trousers** for dismounted troops, reaching below the knee, where they are confined by puttees.

12 - M1912 natural leather hobnailed **boots**.

13 - M1941 Carcano **rifle** in 6.5 mm calibre - a slightly modified development of the old M1891.

RED ARMY INFANTRYMAN, WINTER 1941

The uniforms of the Red Army underwent a radical process of reform in the years following 1918, when a conscious effort was made to turn away from imperial traditions. In 1936 a new, predominantly light brown uniform was adopted. Of a modern and practical cut, its shortcomings were however revealed by the campaign against Finland in 1939. This 'Winter War' cost thousands of Soviet lives through the failure to provide adequate protection against the cold, which often fell to 40° below zero. An efficient cold weather garment, the 'Tielogreika,' was later mass-produced. The first issues of this padded suit proved their worth in the savage winter of 1941-42, when the Wehrmacht's lightning drive into the heart of Russia was halted before Moscow. German troops, dressed only in the woollen uniforms suitable for a mild winter, faced Soviet reinforcements trained, and suitably equipped, in Siberia.

1 - M1940 Shapka-ushanka **cap** in fleece trimmed cloth, which replaced the pointed 'Budionovka' bonnet of the Civil War. The Ushanka was popular and efficient; it was even worn under the steel **helmet**, and was copied by the German Wehrmacht and later by many other armies. The officers' version had real fur trim, the other ranks' artificial fur (popularly known as 'fish fur' !)

2 - Enamelled red star **badge**; a plain green painted version was also used from 1942.

3 - The M1941 'Tielogreika' **jacket**, in quilted light brown cloth. At this date it was not generally available, and was much sought after. Its simple, roomy design was highly efficient for field wear in the coldest climates. Manufactured – like most Soviet uniform items – at factories dispersed all over the USSR, it appeared with a number of slightly varying designs of pockets, buttons, collar and wrist tabs, etc.

4 - Trousers, made in the same quilted material as the jacket. These were rather less often seen, perhaps because some soldiers found them cumbersome. There were wide colour variations between jackets and trousers, from yellowish brown to greenish brown.

5 - Standard **belt** in natural leather, with a single prong buckle; this item was virtually unchanged since before the Revolution.

6 - Holster for the Nagant M1895 7.62 mm revolver. Although completely out of date by 1941 this was still the regulation sidearm of many officers, some NCOs and specialists, such as signallers, machine gunners, drivers, etc. Il was slowly replaced by the Tokarev TT33 pistol, which was first issued during the 1939 war against Finland.

7 - Map case in natural leather issued to officers, NCO section commanders and reconnaissance personnel; there were many variations of material and detail design.

8 - Black leather boots, a pattern more than a century-old. In very cold weather they were often replaced by felt 'Valenki' boots, which could be stuffed with insulating material.

9 - Carrier for the drum magazine of the PPSh41 sub-machine gun, in yellow-brown canvas.

10 - PPSh41 **submachine gun**, designed by the engineer Shpagin and suitable for mass-production. This robust, reliable weapon became the trademark of the Red army soldier. Although supplies only allowed its issue to the pick of front line troops in 1941, some five million were made during the war. Together with the later PPD43, it became the weapon of about one infantryman out of three. It fired standard 7.62 mm pistol ammunition, and the drum accommodated 71 rounds. The combination of short practical range and high rate of fire accorded with the aggressive combat doctrine encouraged by the Russian command.

GERMAN MACHINE GUNNER, RUSSIA, SUMMER 1943

After four years of war, the outline of the German frontline infantryman had undergone a noticeable change. The basic uniforms and equipment were still those of 1939, but there now appeared the first sizeable issues of camouflage combat smocks and helmet covers, following the trend set by the Waffen-SS since 1938. The equipment actually carried in the assault was lighter than ever: the German infantryman was able to leave much of his kit in unit transport during actual combat. The soldier illustrated is a light machine gunner, and carries on his person all necessary special equipment for this function. Each infantry section had at least one LMG.

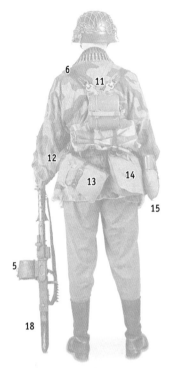

1 - M1942 steel **helmet**, a simplified version of the M1935. To ease mass production, the shell edge was not crimped, and turned outwards.

2 - Regulation **camouflage net**, issued from 1942. It could be fashioned in various shapes to break the outline of the helmet, thanks to small metal wire hooks.

3 - Camouflage **smock** in the Army 'splinter' pattern, first adopted for the 'Zeltbahn' tent section in 1931. Designed to be worn over the uniform, the smock was of loose cut, tightened by elasticated tapes at the wrists, by laces at the neck and tapes at the waist. Some smocks also feature vertical slits on the chest, giving access to the pockets of the woollen tunic.

4 - **Belt** of 150 linked 7.92 mm cartridges.

5 - M1934 50-round **drum magazine,** used on the LMG for assaults and other occasions when the belt would be inconvenient.

6 - M1939 infantry **equipment suspenders**, in leather with matt grey metal fixtures. Normally engaged with the rifleman's cartridge pouches, they could also support alternative items carried on the belt, as here.

7 - Black leather **belt**, with the Army's grey painted buckle.

8 - **Accessory pouch** for the MG34 light machine gun: it contains an anti-aircraft sight, an extractor tool, an oil can, a spare breechblock, a belt feeder tongue, a flash-hider, a protective glove for changing hot barrels, and various maintenance and cleaning tools.

9 - Standard issue **flashlight**.

10 - **Holster** for the pistol issued to machine gunners as their personal sidearm - here, the Walther P38 9-mm automatic.

11 - **Assault pack webbing frame**, hooked onto the equipment suspenders. Several straps held minimal field equipment: such as the mess tin, the rolled Zeltbahn, and a special pouch containing iron rations, tent pegs, etc.

12 - M1938 **gasmask** in its painted metal canister, here of the second (lengthened) type.

13 - Pocket for the **anti-gas cape**, usually strapped to the gasmask canister although this was officially forbidden.

14 - M1931 **bread bag**, containing small personal items, field cap, rations, etc. Il was carried looped to the belt.

15 - M1931 **water bottle**, with a later pattern cup in enamelled iron painted olive green. The bottle was hooked and strapped onto the bread bag flap.

16 - Field grey wool **trousers**. Of straight cut, these were unchanged since the beginning of the war, apart from their dull green shade instead of stone grey.

17 - Black leather **marching boots**, or 'dice shakers,' their height slightly reduced at the end of 1939.

18 - MG34 **machine gun**, the basic automatic weapon of the infantry section. This should properly be termed a 'general purpose' machine gun; it was more sophisticated and much faster-firing than the magazine-fed LMGs of Allied armies, and when fitted to a tripod mount could perform all the fixed firing tasks of a medium machine gun.

RED ARMY RIFLEMAN, SUMMER 1943

On 15 January 1943 Stalin signed the regulations known as 'Prikaz 25' of the National Defence Commissariat, which detailed, in 64 pages, the Red Army's new uniforms. This document marked an astonishing about-face, in that it revived significant uniform features from the Tsarist era that had been suppressed since the Revolution. At a time of repeated set backs at the hand of the invaders and millions of casualties, the Soviet regime consciously summoned up the ancient patriotic spirit of the Motherland. The revived prestige of the soldier's uniform had a positive effect on the morale of the 'Frontovik.'

1 - M1935 'Pilotka.' This light brown cotton **side cap**, worn tilted to the right, was the everyday headgear of the Soviet ranker in temperate weather. All enlisted ranks wore the red enamelled star badge, or its field equivalent in green-painted metal since 1942.

2 - The traditional 'Gymnastierka' **shirt-tunic**, M1943. The standard garment in temperate weather, this brown-green canvas pullover blouse had a stand collar closed by two small buttons. This soldier displays the Medal of Military Valour: in the traditional Russian style, medals were displayed even in combat.

3 - M1943 **shoulder boards**. These were of brown wool, piped in the arm-of service colour (raspberry red for infantry, or more properly, 'rifles').

4 - Standard issue **leather belt**.

5 - M1930 **cartridge pouches**, the two pockets each containing three 5-round clips of 7.62 mm ammunition for the rifle.

6 - M1940 **helmet**, which replaced the M1936 type distinguished by its crest. Of very modern shape, this helmet remained in use decades after the war.

7 - Tan canvas bag for the new BN **gasmask**.

8 - M1935 'Sharovari' universal issue cotton **breeches**. Note the characteristic pointed reinforcement patches on the knees.

9 - Standard issue black **leather boots**.

10 - M1939 **knapsack** meant to replace the old soft 'Mieshok' pack, but the latter was still seen in large numbers. The knapsack was made of canvas, and leather or webbing for the binding and tabs. The shoulder straps hooked to rings on the back of the cartridge pouches. Underarm straps held the pack against the soldier's back.

11 - 'Plashtch-palatka' **tent section**, which could be used as a hooded rain cape. A slit on the right side made it possible to slip an arm through when it was worn over the equipment. It is here rolled horsehoe style over the knapsack. The greatcoat could be carried in the same way.

12 - Square-headed **entrenching tool** in its canvas carrier; there were many slightly varying types in simultaneous use.

13 - Aluminium **water bottle** in a canvas carrier looped to the belt.

14 - M1891/30 Mosin Nagant 7.62 mm **rifle**. The 1930 variant of a line of weapons stretching back to the last century was modelled on the 1891 dragoon carbine, shorter than the contemporary infantry rifle. It stayed in service right up to the end of World War II despite being seriously outclassed by more modern designs. Many Soviet soldiers received either the PPSh 41 submachine gun or the semi-automatic Tokarev SVT-40 rifle. The old Mosin Nagant was provided with a cruciform needle bayonet, but seldom with a scabbard. If the bayonet was issued it was carried fixed at all times, here reversed as a safety measure.

WAFFEN-SS INFANTRYMAN, RUSSIA, SUMMER 1943

Raised from the pre-war 'Schütz-Staffel' militia, the Waffen-SS evolved during the war years into what was almost a 'parallel army,' organised into more than 30 divisions - some of them the largest, best-equipped, and most formidable combat formations in the Wehrmacht. Their field grey uniforms were similar to those of the Army apart from their insignia. Committed on the hottest spots of the front as shock troops, the Waffen-SS were the first German soldiers to wear camouflage uniforms, ever since before the war. Camouflage suits and helmets covers would become their trademark. Seven known patterns of camouflage were used during the war, but the 'pea pattern' shown here was the most commonplace. The cloth was reversible, printed on one side with brown shades (autumn colours) and green shades (spring) on the other.

1 - M1935 steel **helmet**. The characteristic camouflage cover was made from no less than 14 separate pieces and held to the shell by three spring hooks which engaged at sides and rear. This is a first type cover, lacking the external loops for foliage.

2 - Only the collar of the Feldgrau **field tunic** is seen above the camouflage smock. It bears the SS collar patches, in the form of black cloth rhomboids. The right side tab bears the SS runes woven in white thread for other ranks; the left side tab has the twin stripes of a senior corporal.

3 - Camouflage smock. Of loose cut, gathered at wrist, waist and neck by elastics or laces, it was worn over the woollen uniform but under the equipment. The first smocks were tested as early as 1938. This is the last pattern, manufactured in 1942-44, with two skirt pockets, and chest opening down to the waist. Another sign of a late-pattern smock is the series of foliage loops sewn onto the shoulders and arms. Here both smock and helmet cover display the green-dominant 'spring' side.

4 - M1939 black leather **infantry equipment suspenders**.

5 - Standard issue black leather rifle **cartridge pouches**, two sets of three, holding a total of 12 five round clips of 7.92 mm Mauser ammunition.

6 - M1924 **hand grenade**.

7 - Standard issue **black leather belt**, the plate of grey-painted metal bearing a design peculiar to the SS: an eagle with outstretched wings, clutching a swastika, the wings breaking a riband bearing the motto 'My Honour Is Loyalty.'

8 - M1884/98 **bayonet** in an old-pattern black leather frog (without hilt strap).

9 - Folding **entrenching shovel**, in its metal-reinforced leather carrier, which included a loop for the bayonet scabbard.

10 - M1938 **gasmask** in its painted metal canister.

11 - Anti-gas cape, here in a late type of pouch made in ordinary (i.e. non - proofed) cloth.

12 - Zeltbahn **tent section** in the specific WSS camouflage pattern, here simply strapped to the belt - a common practice when in light fighting order.

13 - M1931 **water bottle**, with mid-war enamelled iron cup painted olive green

14 - M1931 **bread bag.**

15 - M1942 tapered leg **trousers** in field grey cloth. These had belt loops; tapes and foot straps at the bottom of each leg, introduced for use with field shoes and web anklets.

16 - Canvas **anklets**, with leather tabs.

17 - Ankle boots in natural leather, first issued to some troops in 1937, replaced the high boots during the war years for economy reasons. Usually blacked in use, they sometimes appeared in natural tan.

18 - Karabiner 98k 7.92 mm **rifle**.

4
12
10   11
13
14

JAPANESE INFANTRYMAN, SUMMER 1942

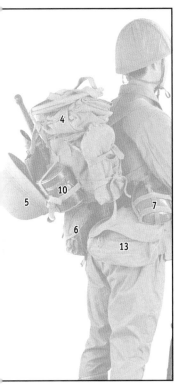

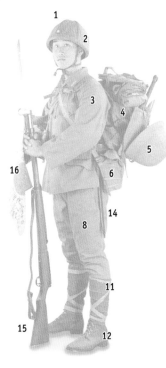

At the time of Japan's entry into the world war on 7 December 1941, the Japanese infantryman was equipped with an outfit which had benefitted from prolonged field experience in Manchuria and China. In 1941-42, he wore the Model 98 uniform, introduced in 1938. This was made in both brown wool for winter and lighter cotton for summer and tropical use. The 'Hetai,' as the Emperor's footslogger was known, confronted Allied forces in Asia and the Pacific in this simple uniform. The model illustrated here wears summer dress with complete marching kit. In accordance with tradition, he carries a flag presented to him by his family.

1 - Model 92 (1932) **helmet**, introduced during the Chinese campaign; the pot-shaped steel shell, painted khaki-brown, rested on the head over small adjustable pads. The frontal insignia was in the form of a star for the Army.

2 - **Helmet** cover, in khaki quilted linen, with a yellow star sewn onto a round piece of uniform cloth.

3 - 98 Pattern **tunic** (1938), in cotton for tropical wear. It has five front buttons, two hip vents, a tab to support the belt on the left where the bayonet was slung, and four buttoned pockets. Collar patches bore the insignia of rank, here those of a private first class.

4 - Rectangular canvas **knapsack**, with cloth tapes retaining the exterior load: a canvas water carrier, the raincoat and tent section (which could be worn as a poncho) rolled together in horseshoe fashion, spare boots, and the spade, its head removed from the haft and carried in a cloth cover.

5 - Tropical **helmet**. There were a number of different types; this one is made of cork with a cotton cover. There was also a soft version, which the soldier could wear under his steel helmet.

6 - **Gasmask**, similar in design to the British service respirator.

7 - M1933 **waterbottle**, in brown-painted aluminium. A strap of the carrier passed through a ring on the stopper.

8 - **Trousers**, slightly flared at the thigh, cut from khaki cotton. They were gathered at the ankle by means of buttons, laces or press-studs.

9 - Natural leather **belt** with a single-prong buckle.

The three cartridge pouches in natural leather slipped over the belt. The front pair held 30 rounds each; the larger, rear pouch held 60 rounds and the rifle cleaning kit. The bayonet frog, also in natural leather, was placed on the left.

10 - **Mess tin** in brown-painted aluminium, strapped to the pack.

11 - **Puttees** were made of either winter or summer weight uniform cloth; note how the end tapes were bound in an 'X' pattern, characteristic of the Japanese.

12 - Standard issue **ankle boots** in natural leather.

13 - Cloth **sidebag** for personal effects.

14 - Quillon **bayonet** for the Model 38 Arisaka rifle.

15 - Model 38 **rifle**, named after its inventor, Col. Nariaki Arisaka. In service with the Japanese Army from 1906 to 1945, this was a 6.5 mm weapon which appeared in both 'long' and 'short' models - though at 44ins., even the 'short' type was unwieldy enough in thick jungle.

16 - The 'Buun-Tchokyu,' a patriotic **good luck flag** inscribed by the soldier's family and friends with prayers for honour and good fortune.

US MARINE, MARIANA ISLANDS, JUNE 1944

The crack infantry of the US Marine Corps were considered part of the US Navy. Their tactical employment, and details of their clothing and equipment, also distinguished them from the bulk of United States servicemen. They specialised in amphibious assault, and were employed almost exclusively in the Pacific theatre of operations. During the savage and costly counteroffensive against the Japanese, which lasted three and a half years, they became renowned for their fighting qualities and their tenacity, at a heavy cost in lives. Our subject is a sniper from the 2nd Marine Division. The Japanese were adept at last-ditch defence of cunningly concealed positions, and their snipers added to the attackers' hardships. Marines were obliged to put much effort into locating and neutralising them.

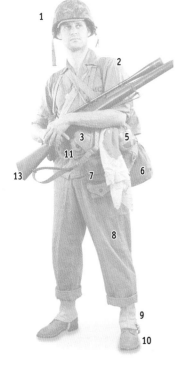

1 - Standard M1 steel **helmet,** here with the cloth camouflage cover peculiar to the US Marines; like other camouflaged items, it was predominantly brown and tan on one side, and green on the other, being theoretically reversible for operations on beaches or in the jungle. The light green 'Utility' **cap** was often worn under the helmet.

2 - 1941 Pattern **Utility jacket,** in light green herringbone twill. It has three patch pockets without flaps, the USMC acronym and emblem (eagle, globe and anchor) being stencilled on the left breast pocket. The front and cuffs are fastened with brass tack buttons. The oval shaped metal identity discs ('dog tags') hang from the neck on a lace.

3 - Ammunition **bandolier,** a throw-away item issued already packed with 12 clips for the rifle. The strap length is adjusted thanks to a safety pin.

4 - The Marine Corps 1941 pattern pack system consisted of a **haversack,** which is worn alone here for combat, and a knapsack, which could be attached below. The M1910 T-handled shovel is hooked to the flap. The camouflaged poncho, in coated canvas, is rolled up and tied round the haversack.

5 - War booty: a Japanese water bottle and flag. Such souvenirs were prized, and could be traded with rear-echelon personnel for cash, liquor, or other comforts.

6 - M4 bag for the M6 lightweight **gasmask,** an Army issue item.

7 - M-2 **Jungle first aid kit** hooked to the belt. It contains, among other supplies, a bottle of insect repellent and a cure for foot fungus. The standard M-1924 first aid packet pouch is hooked under it.

8 - 1941 Pattern Utility **trousers,** in the same material as the jacket. They had two slanted front pockets and two patch rear pockets, and tack fly buttons.

9 - Marine Corps **leggings,** which had fewer eyelets than the Army type. In the Pacific, the trousers were often worn loose or rolled.

10 - Service shoes ('Boondockers'), in 'rough side out' leather, rubber heels and soles.

11 - Webbing M1923 **cartridge belt,** consisting of ten pouches with snap studs, each containing two clips of .30 calibre rounds. The Marine Corps webbing suspenders attached to the belt eyelets with snap hooks at the back and open hooks at the front. A Mark II fragmentation grenade is carried with its lever hooked through the ring of one suspender. The water bottle **(12)** in its specific 'crossed flaps' carrier, and a leather-sheathed fighting knife, are also hooked to the lower eyelets.

13 - Springfield M1903A4 **rifle** with telescopic sights. The old bolt-action Springfield was preferred, over the semi-automatic M1 Garand rifle which armed most Marines, for sniping work: rate of fire was less important than accuracy.

JAPANESE INFANTRYMAN, SPRING 1944

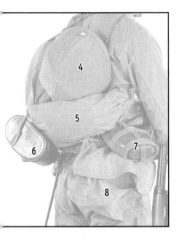

The simple, lightweight Japanese uniform was from the first quite suitable for tropical campaigning, and underwent little change during the war years. As wartime shortages began to bite there was a certain amount of substitution of nonstrategic materials, however: many leather items were replaced with cheaper equivalents made of vulcanised fibre or rubberised cloth. This soldier is wearing the lightened equipment typical of the jungle campaigns. The cap, shirt, and 'horseshoe roll' containing basic necessities were characteristic of the defenders of the Pacific Islands against the US forces, and of Burma against the British 14th Army. Although some issue items - e.g. the gasmask - have been discarded as useless encumbrances, he still carries, fixed to his bayonet, the good luck flag presented by his family.

1 - Field cap in light cloth, introduced in 1938; manufactured in various materials, it was the most characteristic headgear of the Japanese soldier. It always bore on the front the yellow star of the Army. The example illustrated has an 'economy' chin strap, and tightens at the rear by means of a lace.

2 - Neck flap, hooked to the cap in the Tropics; it is made from four rectangles of cloth.

3 - Cotton shirt, normally worn under a tunic, but worn alone in hot climates; it buttons all the way down the front, and has two breast pockets. Rank insignia were fixed above the left pocket - here, that of a private first class.

4 - Model 1932 steel **helmet**, with its quilted cloth sun-cover (which also bears the yellow star badge). The helmet was often worn on top of the field cap.

5 - Horseshoe roll of spare clothes and basic necessities: a less encumbering way of carrying equipment than the issue knapsack, and one adopted by many armies over the centuries. Although the roll cover was regulation issue, it could also be fashioned out of the tent section.

6 - Mess tin of brown-painted aluminium, strapped to the equipment roll.

7 - Final pattern **water bottle**, in brown-painted aluminium, in its webbing carrier.

8 - Canvas **sidebag**, containing the bare minimum of personal items, washing kit, eating utensils, minimal rations, etc.

9 - The soldier has a real **leather belt**, but his ammunition pouches are made of vulcanised fibre, typical of the later part of the war; fabric belts were also common.

10 - This **cloth bag**, marked with ideograms, contains the soldier's most valued possessions and his personal documents.

11 - Cotton flared **trousers,** gathered at the ankle by buttons or laces. The cut of these trousers varied, from actual jodhpurs to a straighter leg.

12 - Puttees, of either heavy wool or light cotton cloth.

13 - Standard issue natural **leather boots**. In the tropics these were often replaced by the 'Jikatabi,' light field shoes in canvas and rubber, with a separate big toe.

14 - Model 38 Arisaka **rifle** - the number referring to the 38th year of Emperor Meiji's dynasty, or 1906. There was an attempt to replace this outdated 6.5 mm calibre weapon with the newer Model 99 in the 7.7 mm calibre already employed by the Model 92 machine gun, but this was never achieved, and the confusion of calibres made for logistical difficulties.

US ARMY INFANTRYMAN, OKINAWA, MAY 1945

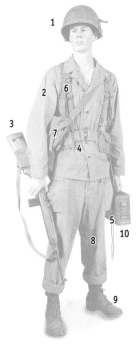

This enlisted man is dressed like the majority of the US Army fighting in the Pacific in the closing months of the war. The special demands on uniform and equipment made by campaigning in the tropics were the subject of extensive technical studies. After the limited issue of camouflage uniforms, which were uncomfortable and disliked by the GI's, the Army reverted to the less conspicuous and more comfortable green 'fatigue' outfit. This 96th Infantry division soldier is a machine gun team ammunition carrier taking part in the very harsh fighting on Okinawa.

1 - M1 **steel helmet** with the neoprene band introduced in 1943 with a machine-made camouflage net. The shell chin strap is tucked under the former.

2 - 1942 Pattern Herringbone twill (HBT) **jacket**; originally a working and training uniform, these 'fatigues' quickly became the standard combat clothing for hot weather and climates. This pattern is identifiable by the large expandable chest pockets. It is unlined, and was often worn hanging loose over the trousers. The buttons were tack buttons of black metal, or sometimes sewn-on plastic buttons; the straight cuffs had two buttonholes for adjusting the closure.

3 - M1 **carbine** with 15-round magazine. This light weapon was originally designed to replace the M1911A1 automatic pistol; it was issued among others to officers and mortar and MG teams. A magazine pocket is slipped over the stock for quick access.

4 - Webbing equipment. The M1936 pistol belt supports, at the front:
– two carbine magazine pockets, one of which (at right) is also suitable for M1 rifle clips
– on the left side, an M3 trench knife, issued to all personnel armed with the carbine.
And on the back, from left to right:
– the M2 Jungle first aid kit with an M1942 first aid dressing pouch hooked under it

– two M1910 water bottles, on either side of the M-1943 folding entrenching tool
– multi-purpose lightweight poncho in coated nylon, tied to the belt.

6 - Webbing equipment suspenders, an improvement of the M1936, with thick canvas pads over the shoulders and larger rings

7 - M4 bag for the M6 lightweight gas mask.

8 - 1942 pattern HBT **trousers**, with large expandable thigh pockets and tack or plastic buttons. Note the faded colour, due to prolonged exposure to sun, and washing.

9 - Boots, service, combat, aka 'buckle boots,' introduced in 1943 to replace the service shoe and legging combination.

10 - M1 **ammunition can** in stamped metal for machine gun ammunition, holding a 250-round fabric belt, with one tracer every five 'ball' rounds.

FRENCH INFANTRYMAN, VICHY FRANCE, SUMMER 1942

After the Armistice of June 1940 the new Vichy government was permitted to retain a small army for maintaining internal order and protecting overseas colonial territories. The bulk of this force were still dressed as they had been in 1939-40, but a new uniform, the 1941 pattern, began to be manufactured and issued in summer 1942. In November 1942, after the Allied landings in French North Africa and the German occupation of the French 'Free Zone,' the Army of the Armistice inside France was disbanded. The African garrisons rallied to the Allies, forming the core of the Army of Liberation. The 1941 uniform continued to be made during 1943-44, and was issued to various units, including the '1er régiment de France;' the Milice (who received the dark blue version intended for the Chasseurs light infantry); and in autumn 1944, to the Maquis units and the new regiments which were committed alongside the Allies in the last winter of the war.

1 - Steel **helmet** M1926, with M1937 emblem embossed on a metal disc. The new 1941 set of issue had been intended to include a helmet with a small metal crest and a front buffer, like those of the motorised troops, but it never appeared.

2 - 1941pattern **shirt and tie**. The shirt differed from the M1935 type mainly in having shoulder straps; the tie was tapered and ending in a point, whereas the old tie had been straight and square-ended.

3 - 1941 pattern **tunic**. Originally this had been intended only for a walking-out and parade item, and a canvas jacket – modelled on those used by the ski troops in the Norwegian campaign of 1940 – had been planned for field wear. In practice the latter could not be manufactured, so the tunic became an all-purpose garment. Its cut was similar to an officer's tunic, with an open collar and four pockets; removable 'rolled' shoulder straps were added for campaign use, and the cuffs were buttoned to allow them to be turned up in warm weather. The fourragere in the colour (red) of the Légion d'Honneur was worn by the 1er régiment de France. Its collar patches bear the numeral 1 and pipings in the new infantry colour - crimson - as per the 1942 regulations.

4 - 1935 pattern **equipment**, unchanged since 1939-40. No gasmask is carried as its issue was forbidden under the terms of the Armistice with the Germans.

5 - Model of 1941 **trousers.** Of straight cut, they were designed to be worn loose at the ankle in walking-out dress. The cloth, of the same brown shade as the tunic, was of inferior quality, and tended to turn greyish with use.

6 - 1941 pattern **leggings**. A limited issue of front-lacing anklets had been made to the infantry in spring 1940, replacing the old puttees. The 1941 model were taller and more rigid, with side fastenings and a bill covering the lacing.

7 - 1941 pattern **service shoes** in a new 'derby' shape and hardened, rounded toe.

8 - MAS 36 **rifle**; enough remained after the Armistice to equip the whole Vichy army, which had slightly less than 100,000 men.

© Histoire & Collections

BRITISH BREN GUNNER, SICILY, JULY 1943

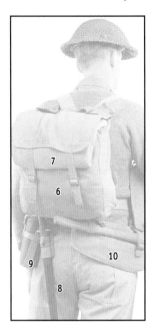

After the final victory in North Africa in May 1943, the British 8th Army landed in Sicily as a necessary prelude to an invasion of the Italian mainland. Montgomery's desert veterans, drawn from many Commonwealth nations and fighting alongside French, Polish and Canadian comrades as well as the American 5th Army, now faced a slow, costly, two-year campaign against stubborn and skilled German defenders. In summer, the climate and terrain differed little from that encountered in the last stages of the African campaign, and the 8th Army retained their desert uniforms. The substitution of khaki drill trousers for the shorts was the only major change to the infantryman's silhouette. In the extremely cold, wet Italian mountain winters Battledress was issued, and proved barely adequate in conditions as harsh as anything suffered by the British Army in North-West Europe.

1 - Mark II steel **helmet**, finished with matt light brown paint, and covered with a camouflage net. Photographs show that hessian and/or foliage 'garnish' was applied to this sparingly, if at all, in the Italian theatre.

2 - The 'Aertex' cotton **shirt** in pale khaki, as worn in Africa.

3 - V-neck **sweater** in khaki wool. This was issued in all theatres, and was a useful and comfortable field garment.

4 - 1937 pattern **webbing equipment**, in 'Field Service Marching Order' arrangement. The haversack or 'small pack' worn on the back in 'Battle Order' (not worn here) usually moved to the left hip, where it was attached to the brace ends; and the 'large pack' or valise – an item retained from the old 1908 pattern equipment – was worn on the back instead. It was attached by means of the same removable L-shaped straps as the small pack in this position; the hooks at the angle of the 'L' engaged with the buckles of the universal pouches. The Large Pack contained changes of underwear, shirt, socks, etc., spare boots, canvas and rubber plimsolls, and personal kit; washing kit, towel, groundsheet/rain cape, and other necessities were divided between large and small packs when both were carried. In actual combat the valise was left with the unit transport, together with greatcoats and blankets if they were not immediately needed. The bayonet was not compatible with a light machine gun, but was used on campaign for 'camp chores' or for mine-probing. Note the issue jackknife hanging from the belt with its lanyard.

5 - Water bottle, unchanged since 1905. There were two types of carrier, one a complete 'pocket' and the other in open strapwork. The bottle had been intended to be carried in the small pack, but the addition of extra items of kit to the soldier's load meant that it was almost invariably moved to the belt to make room in the haversack.

6 - Entrenching tool, its steel mattock head carried in the webbing pocket and its haft buckled across the outside.

7 - Khaki drill full-length **tropical trousers,** which began to be issued to all troops in this theatre. They were modelled on the Battledress trousers in that they too had the large (left thigh) map pocket and small (right hip) first field dressing pocket.

8 - Bren Mark I **light machine gun**, .303 in. calibre. This was the infantry section's automatic weapon, and each ten-man section consisted of a two-man Bren group led by the lance-corporal deputy section leader, and six riflemen led by the corporal section leader. Simple, robust and reliable, and extremely accurate at normal battle ranges, the Bren was a popular weapon. Its 30-round curved box magazines were carried in the universal pouches; the Bren 'No. I' carried four, his 'No.2' four, and the lance-corporal four. Each rifleman also carried two magazines, and these could be passed to the Bren group as needed.

9 - Webbing Anklets, the short buckled gaiters worn by most British troops of all branches of service.

10 - Standard issue hobnailed 'arnmunition **boots'** in black pebbled leather.

BERSAGLIER, ITALIAN SOCIAL REPUBLIC, 1944

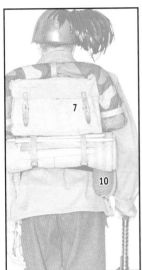

O n 15 September 1943 the Italian Social Republic was created: a puppet Fascist state in German-occupied Italy, and nominally ruled by Mussolini. The army of the RSI was made up of Italian Fascists loyal to Il Duce, drawn from the ranks of the old royal army and the Blackshirt militia. Four divisions strong, this force was largely formed and trained in Germany. At first the RSI troops wore the uniforms of the royal army with the addition of new insignia, the Roman sword being a common emblem. But despite their unenviable military situation and threatening future, the RSI soon produced quite a range of new outfits which, together with a mixture of old uniforms, camouflage garments and German items, gave the Fascist troops a characteristic appearance. The soldier illustrated is a senior corporal of Bersaglieri light infantry in the newly formed 'Italia' Division.

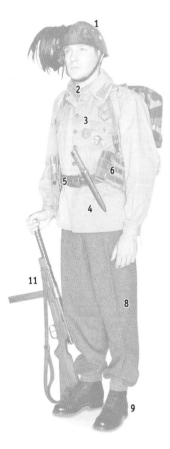

1 - M1933 steel **helmet**; unchanged in form, it is here with camouflage paint, a tricolour insignia, and the Bersaglieri black cock's feathers.

2 - M1939 grey-green flannel **shirt**.

3 - M1940 **windjacket**, in grey-brown windproof material. Originally part of the Alpini and Bersaglieri set of clothing, it was more widely distributed late in the war. It has a fall collar, two buttoned pockets, and six front buttons. The crimson collar 'flames' of the Bersaglieri bear the Roman sword and wreath of the RSI in place of the star of the old royal army. The red and gold rank chevrons are stitched above the left breast pocket. Below the rank badge is an RSI volunteers' badge, with the unofficial death's-head badge popular among Mussolini's last fanatics.

4 - **Bayonet/dagger** for the MAB38a sub-machine gun, with a folding blade, and a hilt-hook which kept it at this tilted angle on the belt.

5 - 1944 pattern **belt**, an obvious copy of the German type, the buckle plate bearing an eagle and fasces emblem.

6 - **Magazine pouches**, also copied from German models; the body was made of canvas, with leather flaps and straps. Each pouch carried three box magazines. The **suspender** is the old M1891 type - a good example of the mixture of old and new in RSI equipment.

7 - M1939 rectangular **knapsack**, with the blanket and camouflaged tent section/poncho rolled and strapped to it.

8 - M1941 paratrooper **trousers**. These grey-green trousers were cut straight, and fastened at the ankle with buttoned tabs or laces. They are tucked into the socks in this photograph; as they were often without any sort of puttees or gaiters. The paratrooper trousers had two oblique side pockets and two buttoned hip pockets.

9 - Standard issue black leather M1912 **boots**.

10 - Standard issue one-litre aluminium **canteen** with wool cover.

11 - Beretta M1938a **sub-machine gun**. An excellent weapon, prized by any Allied soldier who could lay hands on one. It has two triggers, the front one for single shots and the rear one for bursts. A special cartridge (9 mm 38a) was issued for this weapon, but it would also take the Glisenti 9 mm and German Parabellum 9 mm rounds. Widely used on all fronts by Italian troops, and distributed in large numbers to the RSI forces. Production stopped in 1944 but was resumed in 1950.

GERMAN MOUNTAIN TROOPER, ITALY, SUMMER 1944

Thanks to a clever use of limited manpower and resources, in a terrain which greatly favoured the defence over the attack, the German troops in Italy managed to delay the Allies right up until the end of the war. Although stripped of supplies in favour of the more immediately threatening Western and Eastern Fronts, the troops in Italy fought cunningly and stubbornly, making the Allies pay the highest cost in blood and material before falling back to the next prepared defensive line. In this theatre the troops were equipped with a mixture of the classic field grey 'temperate' uniform, tropical uniform, camouflage items, and confiscated Italian items.

1 - Field grey **mountain cap**, modelled originally on that of the Austrian army of the Great War. The Gebirgsjäger were at first the only troops wearing a peaked field cap; but it was copied in 1941 for the new tropical field cap of the Afrika Korps, and in 1943 a very similar pattern became the universal issue field cap, replacing the side cap. The mountain cap has a slightly higher outline and shorter peak than the later types. There are two ventilation eyelets; and the band, which can be folded down to protect the face, fastens with two front buttons. The eagle-and-swastika badge in grey on green, and the cloth cockade, are displayed on the front of the crown; and the metal branch-of-service badge, an edelweiss flower, is pinned to the left side.

2 - Tropical **shirt** in olive green cotton.

3 - **Tropical tunic**, of the simplified type which appeared in 1942-43, of looser cut and with unpleated pockets. The original olive shade became very faded in use. The usual removable shoulder straps of tropical pattern bear the medium green piping of the mountain troops. The illustrated example of the branch's edelweiss sleeve patch is in tropical pattern, embroidered in white on brown; the Army's breast eagle is in tropical blue and brown. Insignia from the woollen uniform, in standard colours, were often seen on tropical clothing in Italy.

4 - **Equipment suspenders** in yellow-tan webbing, produced for tropical use but often seen in mainland Europe in 1943-45.

5 - **Cartridge pouches** in canvas and leather, each of the pair holding two magazines for the semi-automatic Gewehr 43 rifle; the colours and exact materials varied. These pouches were in short supply, and often a rifleman had to use one pair of canvas pouches for the detachable magazines, and one set of three standard pouches holding loose rounds or clips.

6 - M1942 steel **helmet**, camouflage-painted to match the terrain on this front.

7 - Standard issue black **leather belt**.

8 - M1931 **bread bag**.

9 - **Water bottle**, here the large one-litre version for mountain troops.

10 - Straight-cut cotton **trousers**. They feature two side pockets, one with a buttoned flap on the right rear, and an integral belt with a three-prong buckle.

11 - Wool alpine **puttees** in elasticated cotton, a small hook held them down on the boots.

12 - **Mountain boots**, heavily nailed and cleated, made of natural leather with a top strip of field grey cloth.

13 - Gewehr 43 semi-automatic **rifle**, in 7.92 mm calibre, with a detachable ten-round magazine; this was an efficient weapon, but it was never available in large numbers, and its hurrying into service led to frequent malfunctions.

14 - ZF4 **telescopic sight**, x 4 magnification.

U.S. ARMY AUTOMATIC RIFLEMAN, JUNE 1944

Depicted as he embarks for Normandy, this rifle squad automatic rifleman represents the typical GI of early 1944 in the European Theater of Operations. There had been a certain amount of modification of individual items, and the introduction of some new materials; but the basic outfit had not changed significantly since the entry of the United States into the war.

1 - M1 steel **helmet**, which officially replaced the M1917A1 (of British shape) in June 1941. Apart from its very modern outline, the M1 had another unique feature, its construction in two parts. The outer steel shell, to which the main chin strap was fixed, fitted over a slightly smaller 'Liner' made of laminated fibre. The liner contained an adjustable system of fabric straps which gripped the head. It could be also worn by itself when out of battle. Here the two-part webbing chin strap of the shell (rarely fastened in battle) is tucked into the camouflage net.

2 - The M1941 knitted **woollen cap**, or 'beanie,' was intended be worn under the helmet in cold weather. It has a short stiffened peak, and the sides and rear can be folded down over the ears.

3 - Olive drab **flannel shirt**. It had two patch breast pockets, and could be worn with a necktie in service uniform mode. An internal flap, buttoned behind the front, and sleeve gussets were anti-vesicant gas features.

4 - Olive drab **field jacket**, made of tan poplin and lined with olive green flannel. Introduced in 1941, this windcheater, consciously modelled on civilian sportswear, was an important innovation. It was the first example of an universal issue garment specifically for field wear, replacing the older-style wool tunics. It closes down the front with a zipper covered by a buttoned fly; there are buttoned tabs at the collar, wrists and waist. Two large vertical pleats on the back give easy fitting. The field jacket soon showed its shortcomings, however. It was comfortable in temperate weather, but was too thin in the winter, and too hot in summer; and its two slash pockets had no useful carrying capacity. The example illustrated bears the patch of the 2nd (Indianhead) Infantry Division, which landed on Omaha Beach on D+1 and D+2.

5 - The M1928 **haversack** had inadequate capacity, and it was partially replaced by larger or more elaborate packs later in the war. But few of these new packs had been issued before VE-Day, and most troops soldiered on with the M1928. For an 'administrative' landing, our subject has the uncomfortable 'Pack carrier' attached below the haversack, holding a tent section, poles and pins, blanket and a change of clothes. The haversack itself held 6 ration cans, toiletry kit, raincoat, etc.; the pocket on its flap was for the mess kit and utensils. An M1910 pick is hooked under it. An additional blanket has been tied in horseshoe fashion around the pack, together with a folded US Navy M1926 life preserver and a regulation bugle (Note however that buglers were usually armed with a carbine).

6 - M4 **gas mask** in its M6 bag, an item of equipment that had to be carried at all times. But at the front, the mask was often discarded and its bag retained for personal items.

7 - M1937 **automatic rifleman's belt,** with six pouches each holding two 20-round magazines for the Browning Automatic Rifle. The top row of grommets received the ends hooks of the haversack straps, and the bottom row various carriers, such as the M1924 field dressing pouch at right front, the M1938 wirecutters on the left, and the M1910 water bottle carrier at the rear.

8 - Browning Automatic Rifle, M1918A2, .30 calibre, with its adjustable leather sling.

9 - Olive drab 1937 pattern **serge trousers**. For much of the war the GI wore these all-purpose trousers with the field jacket.

10 - M1938 web **leggings**, laced up the outside and with a strap passing under the service shoe.

11 - 'Rough-out' leather **service shoes**, with reclaimed rubber heel and sole. This intermediate pattern retains a toe cap. For Normandy, the shoe was heavily impregnated with a special anti-vesicant dubbin.

GERMAN INFANTRYMAN, NORMANDY, SUMMER 1944

I n the summer of 1944, fighting on three fronts under skies ruled by the Allies, the Wehrmacht was beginning to suffer from serious shortages. The Landser, though his fighting spirit remained high, presented a picture of forced economy and compromise. His uniform, of simplified cut, was made of mixed fibers. It was less robust than before, and its colour tended more towards a brownish grey than the classic field grey. Leather equipment was increasingly replaced by various 'ersatz' equivalents. By contrast, his weapons were becoming ever more efficient, and he faced the swarming Allied armour with the best infantry antitank weapon of the whole war: the single-shot Panzerfaust.

1 - M1943 **field cap**, bearing the Army insignia and cockade woven on a triangular grey patch. This cap, modelled on the mountain cap but of lower outline and with a longer peak, began to replace the side cap in 1943. The side flap is secured at the front with one or two buttons.

2 - M1943 **shirt**, in grey-green knit material, with a three-button front and two buttoned breast pockets. The shirt collar was usually placed over that of the tunic.

3 - Field grey **tunic**, of 1943/44 manufacture. Simplified for economy, it has unpleated pockets with square-shaped flaps, and a field grey collar in place of the earlier green. The material has a low proportion of wool versus artificial fibers and its colours is greyer. The standard collar tabs are woven in mouse grey over feldgrau, without branch-of-service colour piping. The Army breast eagle above the right pocket is also dull grey on field grey, rather than white on green. The ribbon in his second buttonhole is that of the Iron Cross 2nd Class. The field grey shoulder straps bear white infantry branch piping.

4 - Equipment **suspenders** M1939.

5 - M1933 rifle cartridge **pouches**.

6 - M1924 hand **grenade**.

7 - M1939 'egg' **grenade**.

8 - The M1935 **helmet** has been fitted with a field expedient cover made of reclaimed tent section material, secured by a band cut from an inner tube.

9 - The M1939 **assault pack frame** supports the mess tin and the rolled M1931 Zeltbahn. The latter hides the lower pouch containing iron rations, sweater, tent pegs, etc.

10 - M1938 **gasmask** and gas cape.

11 - M1931 **water bottle** with an early black painted aluminum cup.

12 - M1874 **field shovel**, the artificial leather carrier hangs from the belt, a long strap holds the tool handle as well as the bayonet scabbard.

13 - M1931 **bread bag.**

14 - M1943 **trousers**, baggy at the thigh and tapered at the ankle, with foot straps.

15 - Becoming scarcer and scarcer, the shortened **marching boots** dating from late 1939.

16 - Karabiner 98k **rifle**, 7.92 mm calibre.

17 - Panzerfaust 60 single-shot **antitank rocket launcher.** Its 6 lb. hollow charge could penetrate any tank of the period, and in the Normandy hedgerows and the ruins of European towns, most fighting was at short range. The tube was rested across the shoulder, and the warhead was aimed with simple flip-up sights (painted phosphorescent for night use).

BRITISH INFANTRYMAN, NORMANDY, JUNE 1944

This soldier of the 3rd Infantry Division, one of the first ashore on Sword Beach on 6 June 1944, wears a uniform basically unchanged since 1940, but with certain items of equipment dating from the invasion preparations of 1943, such as the steel helmet, light gas mask and distinctive Battle jerkin.

1 - Steel helmet, Mark III, of the 'tortoise' shape worn by the Tommy until the 1980s. This was developed in 1942, but first seen in any numbers in Normandy; it was issued while stocks of Mark II helmets were still plentiful, and both were worn side by side until the end of the war.

2 - Rubberised canvas groundsheet/rain cape, rolled and tied at the top of the assault jerkin.

3 - 1940 (Austerity) pattern **Battledress blouse** in brown serge, varying from the pre-war model in having unpleated pockets and visible plastic buttons. This man, like many in Normandy, wears a full set of sleeve insignia. At the top is the regimental title, in white on scarlet for line infantry - here, that of the South Lancashire Regiment, whose 1st Battalion served in the division. Below is the formation sign, its triangular sections a reference to '3.' Infantry units wore red felt strips, their number indicating the senior, second, and junior brigades within the division - here, the senior brigade. Below this are corporal's chevrons. All insignia appeared on both sleeves.

4 - Rubberised inflatable **life belt** issued for the landing. It was largely of psychological value, since it would not save a heavily burdened man.

5 - The 1943 Light **respirator** in its bag. Unlike the older type, this had a filter screwed on to the side of the face mask. The bag also contained disposable acetate eyeshields, ointment, anti-misting wipes for the eye pieces, etc.

6 - The short-lived **Battle jerkin** was issued mainly to the initial assault waves for D-Day. It was supposed to give more flexible stowage of necessary equipment, better weight distribution, and the advantage of being put on or discarded in one piece. Of waterproof brown canvas, it could accommodate a great deal of kit in several pockets, sleeves and compartments, closed by loops and toggles. The angled breast pockets held ammunition and magazines for small arms, grenades, or mortar bombs. The spike bayonet **(7)** is slipped in a sleeve on the side of the left hand waist pocket. The top compartment on the back contains rations, mess tin, cutlery and ammunition; the lower back compartment held the entrenching tool head or mortar bombs. Under the latter can be seen a pair of large folding wirecutters **(8).** A machete **(9)** and its leather scabbard are carried in a sleeve on the side of the top compartment, the mug is tied on the outside. This soldier has looped the assault troops' toggle rope **(10)** round his neck and shoulders and a cotton bandoleer **(11)** for rifle clips is carried across the chest.

12 - Rifle No. 4 Mark I*. A development of the classic .303 in. SMLE for easier manufacture, it was a pre-war design but was not issued in numbers until 1942. A short spike bayonet fitted over the protruding muzzle, which was the immediate distinguishing feature. Note that the standard weapon for a corporal section leader was the Sten submachine gun; but it is also likely that an experienced NCO going into battle would prefer the rifle.

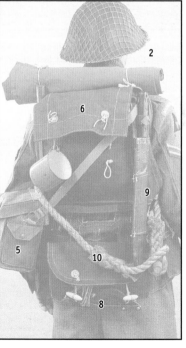

13 - Pattern 1940 **Battledress trousers**. This economy model had exposed pocket buttons, and no belt loops or ankle tabs. The trousers attach to the blouse thanks to three buttons at kidney level. They feature two side pockets, a hip pocket, a first field dressing pocket at front right, and a large patch pocket with buttoned flap on the left thigh front.

14 - Webbing **anklets**, with webbing straps

15 - Hobnailed 'Ammunition **boots.'**

WAFFEN-SS NCO, NORMANDY, SUMMER 1944

T he Allied troops who stormed ashore on D-Day faced variable resistance, some of the German units in coastal defence being of indifferent quality. But the liberators were faced, within hours, by some of the most formidable divisions in the Wehrmacht: first-class Waffen-SS armour and infantry, rushed to the new front as Hitler's 'fire brigade.' Bitterly resisting the Allied advance through the thick hedgerows and small enclosed fields of Normandy, the Waffen-SS made the Allies pay dearly for every yard of French soil. Their appearance represented an ad hoc mixture of the classic uniform items with camouflage garments.

1 - Field grey **side cap**, adopted in 1940, with the Waffen-SS eagle and death's head insignia, woven in silver-grey on black. This cap style had been replaced a year before by the peaked field cap, but was still seen quite widely, particularly among veteran soldiers.

2 - Gray tricot **shirt** with collar, and two buttoned flap breast pockets, introduced in place of the old collarless type in 1943.

3 - Late war pattern **field tunic**, officially field grey, although the shoddy fibre content in the cloth made for colour distortions. Note simplified patch pockets, and field grey collar, characteristic of tunics from 1943 on. The right hand collar patch bears the SS runes; the other the silver star of an 'Unterscharführer.' The collar is edged with the silver-grey NCO braid. On the left upper arm is the SS eagle; on the forearm, the cuff title of the 17th SS Panzer-Grenadier Division 'Götz von Berlichingen.'
On the upper right arm is the award badge for the single-handed destruction of an enemy tank with an infantry weapon, e.g. the Panzerfaust. Unusual for an NCO, the German Cross in Gold is sewn onto the right chest pocket. Also note the whistle lanyard.

4 - Standard M1939 leather **equipment suspenders**.

5 - **Binoculars**, 6x30 magnification, painted in the dull ochre used for German vehicles and many items of equipment from 1943-44.

6 - M1924 **hand grenade**.

7 - Pair of triple **magazine pouches** for the MP40 sub-machine gun, in canvas with leather trim. The left hand set has a small external pocket for tools and loader.

8 - Standard leather **belt** with SS-specific buckle bearing the SS eagle and the motto 'Meine Ehre heisst Treue' - 'My Honour is Loyalty.'

9 - Rubber **lens cover** for the binoculars.

10 - 'Zeltbahn' **shelter half** in SS camouflage pattern.

11 - **Binocular case** in dark brown bakelite.

12 - M1931 **bread bag**.

13 - M1931 **water bottle**.

14 - M1935 steel **helmet**, attached to the belt by its chin strap. The reversible Waffen-SS camouflage cover is the early pattern, without loops for foliage.

15 - **Trousers** in camouflage material, adopted in February 1944. Their cut followed that of the new 1943 wool trousers, fuller in the leg and gathered at the ankle. They could be worn over the latter, or by themselves, as here.

16 - Standard issue gray wool **socks**, here rolled for lack of gaiters.

17 - Standard **ankle boots**; 1937 pattern.

18 - The MP40 **sub-machine gun** in 9 mm calibre, note unfolded skeleton butt.

2ND BATTALION RANGER, NORMANDY, JUNE 1944

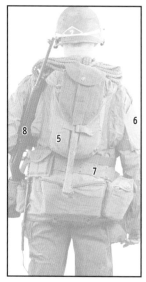

O ur subject represents one of the picked Ranger infantrymen who made the daring assault on the cliff-top battery at Pointe du Hoc, commanding both Utah and Omaha Beaches, on the morning of 6 June. Companies D, E and F of the battalion, commanded by Lieutenant Colonel Rudder, climbed sheer cliffs under heavy fire, captured the battery (from which the 155 mm guns were found to have been removed), and held the position for two days against heavy counterattacks. He wears various equipment specific to the Normandy landings.

1 - M1943 tinted **goggles**, for protection against sun, dust and spray.

2 - M1 steel **helmet**, with the 2nd Ranger Battalion's insignia painted on the back.

3 - M5 amphibious assault **gasmask**. This was a lightweight, short-term use item in a waterproof carrier, to be fixed wherever convenient on the equipment. The carrier also held an acetate protective cover against vesicants, anti-dim cloth, eyeshields and a tube of decontamination ointment.

4 - Olive drab **field jacket** and wool **shirt** (also see page 50). The generic Ranger shoulder patch is sewn at the top of the left sleeve.

5 - Assault vest. The US equivalent of the British 'battle jerkin' (see page 54-55). It features four quick-opening pockets on the front, and two large compartments on the back. Several sets of grommets allow for hooking various items of equipment, such as the folding M-1943 shovel in the back. A coil of rope is tied on top and an M18 smoke grenade is carried in a small pocket on the left waist. Secured at the front by tabs and buckles, the vest can be undone quickly in an emergency.

6 - British gas-detection **brassard**, in a treated paper which changed colour in the presence of sprayed vesicants.

7 - M1936 **pistol belt**, issued to men armed with the pistol or the M1 carbine, it supports various items, hooked to the lower band of grommets, such as: an M1923 double magazine pouch for the automatic Pistol (front left), double magazine pouch for the M1 carbine (back left), M1910 water bottle (back right), M1942 field dressing pouch (front right), M3 knife (left), and M1911A1 .45 cal. pistol in its M1916 holster (right).

8 - M1 carbine, with 20-round magazine.

9 - The M-1942 herringbone twill **trousers** impregnated against vesicants gases and worn over the regular olive drab wool trousers. The capacity of their 'cargo' pockets on the thighs was useful for carrying various paraphernalia.

10 - M1938 canvas **leggings** for dismounted troops.

11 - Standard **service shoes**, with toe cap, reclaimed rubber heels and soles. They were manufactured with the leather rough side out, and impregnated with special antigas dubbin.

WAFFEN-SS INFANTRYMAN, ARDENNES, DECEMBER 1944

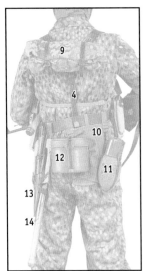

After the Allied break-out from Normandy and the subsequent rapid advance across France, the liberators were checked in Holland and Belgium partly by a revived German resistance, and partly by the fact that they had outrun their armies' ability to supply their massive logistic needs. On 16 December 1944, the German forces launched a last major counter-offensive in the West. Their last reserves were thrown into a drive through the snow-covered Ardennes in Belgium with the aim of reaching Antwerp. A mixture of veterans and new recruits, the assaulting divisions presented a motley appearance, and by no means all of them were properly equipped for winter warfare.

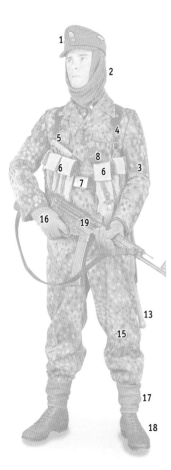

1 - M1943 **field cap**, the Waffen-SS insignia here separated in characteristic fashion, as there was no room for both eagle and death's head on the front above the flap. Some troops received a smaller version of the insignia woven together on a triangular grey patch, worn on the front.

2 - Standard issue 'toque,' a simple woollen tube worn in various ways over the head and neck in cold weather.

3 - Herringbone weave material **camouflage tunic**. Adopted in February 1944 to replace the camo smocks, its cut is identical to the wool tunic's, featuring four patch pockets with square flaps. The camouflage was in the standard 'dot' pattern. The 1944 camo set could be worn over the wool uniform, as here. Shoulder tabs were not normally worn with this tunic.

4 - Standard M1939 **equipment suspenders**.

5 - Wooden-hilted combat **knife**, with a sprung hook on the sheath allowing it to be worn either on a belt or strap, in the boot top, or in the front of the tunic.

6 - Pair of triple **magazine pouches** for the StG 44 assault rifle. They were made in canvas of various shades, often with leather reinforcements. The heavy weight of the six large box magazines - 14 lbs. when fully loaded - required an adjustable strap linking the pouches behind the back, to prevent them falling forward.

7 - Standard **belt** with SS buckle, in silver painted steel.

8 - M1924 **hand grenade.**

9 - Camouflaged **Zeltbahn** tent section, here strapped directly to the D-rings of the equipment suspenders.

10 - M1931 **bread bag.**

11 - M1931 **water bottle**, attached to the bread bag. The cup is in olive painted steel.

12 - Late-war M1931 **mess tin**, in olive painted steel, attached to the bread bag by a black leather strap.

13 - **Entrenching tool** carrier in dull yellow artificial leather. The belt loops and long strap (also retaining the bayonet) are in black leather.

14 - M1884/98 **bayonet**.

15 - **Trousers** of the 1944 SS camouflage uniform (see page 56, fig. 15).

16 - Standard issue grey wool knitted **gloves**.

17 - Grey-green webbing **anklets** with leather tabs.

18 - Standard **ankle boots**.

19 - Sturmgewehr 1944 **assault rifle**, firing special 7.92 mm short rounds. A revolutionary weapon, it was mass-produced from cheap stampings, and therefore vulnerable to hard field use. But inadequate supply of the new ammunition was its main defect.

U.S. ARMY NCO, GERMANY, SPRING 1945

This rifle squad leader wears the new combat uniform adopted in 1943, but which was not issued in large numbers before the end of 1944. Its main characteristics are its deep green colour, the wind and rain resistant material and its adaptability to most climates and seasons thanks to the layering system of added liners and woollens. This outfit became the matrix for the field uniforms of many post-war Western armies.

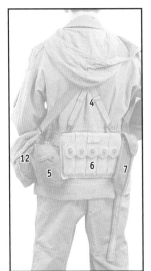

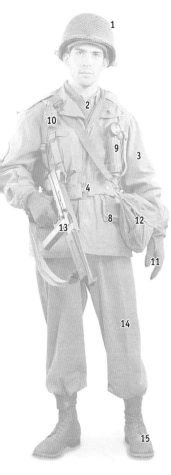

1 - M1 steel **helmet**, covered with the new 1943 factory-made green net and its neoprene band. It is worn over the M1941 wool knit cap.

2 - The **high-neck sweater** with buttoned collar was very popular. It was part of the layering system whereby the field jacket gave protection against wind and rain, warmth being provided by a vest, flannel shirt, and sweater worn underneath.

3 - M1943 **field jacket**. Developed to replace the short field jacket, the tankers,' paratroopers' and mountain troopers' jackets, it has four large pockets; buttoned tabs at the wrist and collar; a fly front; an internal waist tightening cord; and an optional button-on hood. A separate liner jacket in artificial fur – in short supply – could be worn underneath. The shoulder patch (here the yellow Thunderbird of the 45th Infantry Division) is sewn to the left sleeve, the olive drab on dark blue chevrons are those of a Staff Sergeant.

4 - M1936 pistol belt and web **suspenders**. Issued to personnel armed with the pistol or carbine and/or carrying the musette/field bag, the belt and suspenders were also used by other soldiers to support their gear. This is here the M1910 canteen **(5)** in its canvas carrier (note the green shade of US webbing issued as of 1943); a five-magazine carrier **(6)** for the Thompson submachine gun; an M1943 entrenching tool **(7)** and a compass pouch **(8)**. A TL-122C electric torch **(9)** and a Mark II fragmentation grenade **(10)** are hooked to the M1936 suspenders.

11 - Wool **gloves** with leather palm and finger reinforcement.

12 - The M6 carrier for the M4 **gasmask**, which has probably been discarded long ago, leaving the bag to act as a handy 'carry-all.'

13 - Thompson M1A1 .45 calibre **submachine gun**, a simplified version of the M1928A1 most immediately recognisable by the substitution of a plain wooden forearm for the front pistol grip, and the absence of the muzzle compensator. It was partially given to infantry units for patrols, street and house to house fighting.

14 - M1943 **field trousers**, cut like the jacket from green cotton sateen material. They were usually issued one size too large so that they could be worn over the wool trousers, with either belt or suspenders. A buttoning tab gathered the ankle.

15 - M1943 'double buckle' **combat boots**, which began to replace earlier service shoes and leggings in 1944. The cuffs at the ankle are fastened by two buckled straps. Made like the later pattern service shoes from 'rough out' leather, they needed frequent applications of grease to remain adequately waterproof.

GERMAN INFANTRYMAN, BERLIN, APRIL 1945

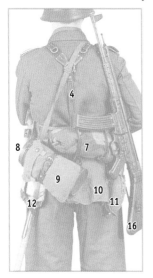

As the shadows closed over the 3rd Reich, the German infantryman presented a very different appearance from his counterpart in the victorious early campaigns. Only the classic helmet remained unchanged. Despite all difficulties, German industry continued to supply the Wehrmacht with equipment, although economy forced radical redesign of some items, with much ersatz material. The final uniform adopted by the Army and Waffen-SS was modelled on British Battledress and economy was the only motive. Various shades of grey cloth were used in its manufacture, including not only German 'shoddy' but also captured Russian and Italian stocks. Only the German soldier's weapons remained of first class quality; and in the ruins of Berlin the StG44 and the Panzerfaust took a high toll of the Red Army.

1 - M1942 steel **helmet**, painted matt grey. Note that the decal insignia had long since been abandoned.

2 - M1943 rayon tricot **shirt** with turn-down collar and two breast pockets.

3 - M1944 **field blouse**, this example made from looted Italian or Czech wool gaberdine. It has two unpleated patch pockets with straight flaps. The shirt collar hides, in this instance, the 'lace' on the collar, which was still of the plain grey design used since 1943. The short blouse has a broad waist band with two buttons. The standard shoulder straps are still attached, here with the white piping of the infantry; and the national eagle is still worn on the right breast, woven in grey thread on a green-grey triangular patch. The ribbon of the Iron Cross 2nd Class is sewn inside the top buttonhole.

4 - M1939 equipment **suspenders** in black leather.

5 - Standard issue **belt and buckle**.

6 - Pair of triple **magazine pouches** for the Sturmgewehr 1944 assault rifle. These appeared in various materials, although the basic design was the same. Khaki-yellow canvas pouches were the most common, although pale blue grey or olive canvas was also used. Closure tabs, loops and trim were of artificial leather or sometimes rubberised fabric.

7 - M1931 camouflaged **tent section**, unchanged throughout the war, held onto the belt by black leather straps.

8 - M1938 **gasmask** in its fluted container. This item, which was completely useless owing to the fact that gas was never used in battle throughout the war, was nevertheless regulation issue until the end of hostilities.

9 - The **anti-gas cape** was equally useless in its intended function; its only practical use was as a makeshift shroud for the dead.

10 - Late example of the M1931 **bread bag**, of simplified construction.

11 - M1931 **water bottle**.

12 - Entrenching **spade** in its dull yellow artificial leather carrier.

13 - M1944 **trousers**, of the same Italian or Czech fabric as the blouse. Of loose cut, with an integral belt, they had two rear pockets, two slash side pockets, and a front fob pocket. Since the M1944 blouse had no internal pocket for the field dressing, this was now carried in the lining of the trousers, on the right side. The legs were gathered at the ankle by a lace.

14 - Canvas **anklets** with leather tabs.

15 - **Ankle boots**.

16 - Sturmgewehr 44 **assault rifle**.

Contents

Note

This book offers only a representative sample of WW2 infantry from the main belligerents. Due to lack of space, for instance, infantry from the Commonwealth countries could not be shown.

Acknowledgments

The assembly of such a large number of original World War II uniforms and equipment items would have been impossible without the generous help of many collections, private and public. We therefore wish to express our gratitude for their co-operation to:

– French Army: Eric Hernandez and François Vauvillier

– British Army and US Armed forces: Jacques Alluchon, Pierre Besnard ('Le Poilu' shop in Paris), Jean Bouchery, Eric Bouteloup, Hubert de Belleville, Philippe Charbonnier, Christophe Deschodt, Raphaël Destombes, Frédéric Finel ('Overlord' shop in Paris), Hervé Halfen, Régis Le Cap, Christian Lefèvre, Eric Martin, Jean-Yves Nasse, Olivier Reinbold, Jean Rocheteau, Hugues Rougé and Nicolas Bellenger

– German army: Eric Lefèvre and Jean de Lagarde (†)

– Italian Army: Furio Lazzarini and Franco Mesturini

– Soviet and Japanese Armies: Gérard Gorokhoff

– Belgian Army: the Musée Royal de l'Armée (Brussels) and Philippe Vernimmen

– Polish army: Daniel Blanchard, Titus and Simon Deleyrolle

Photos credits

Philippe Charbonnier: page 5, 41; Toni Bergamo: 15, 21, 25, 47; Stefan Ciejka: 7, 17, 23, 27, 29, 31, 33, 35, 39, 53, 57, 61, 65; Laurent Mirouze: 11, 13, 19, 37, 45, 49, 51, 55, 59, 63; François Vauvillier: 9, 43.

Histoire & Collections

Series editor Philippe Charbonnier - Design and layout by Philippe Charbonnier et Nathalie Sanchez for *Histoire & Collections*
© *Histoire & Collections 2015*

ISBN: 978-2-35250-340-8

Publisher's number: 35250

© Histoire & Collections 2015

HISTOIRE & COLLECTIONS
5, avenue de la République
75011 Paris - FRANCE
Tél: +33 (0) 1 40 21 18 20 - Fax: +33 (0) 1 47 00 51 11
www.histoireetcollections.com

This book has been designed, typed, laid-out and processed by Histoire & Collections on fully integrated computer equipment.

Printed by Pulsio, Bulgaria, European Union.
April 2015.